LET'S TALK ABOUT RACE

By Julius Lester
Illustrated by Karen Barbour

HarperCollinsPublishers

Amistad

Amistad is an imprint of HarperCollins Publishers. Let's Talk About Race
Text copyright © 2005 by Julius Lester Illustrations copyright © 2005
by Karen Barbour Manufactured in China. All rights reserved. No part
of this book may be used or reproduced in any manner whatsoever
without written permission except in the case of brief quotations
embodied in critical articles and reviews. For information address
HarperCollins Children's Books, a division of
HarperCollins Publishers,
195 Broadway, New York, NY 10007.
www.harpercollinschildrens.com

Library of Congress Cataloging-in-Publication Data   Lester, Julius. Let's
talk about race / by Julius Lester ; illustrated by Karen Barbour.— 1st
ed.   p.   cm.   Summary: The author introduces the concept of race as only
one component in an individual's or nation's "story."
ISBN 978-0-06-028596-8 (trade bdg.) — ISBN 978-0-06-028598-2 (lib. bdg.)
ISBN 978-0-06-446226-6 (pbk.) 1. United States—Race relations—Juvenile
literature. 2. Racism—United States—Juvenile literature. 3. Race
awareness—United States—Juvenile literature. 4. Prejudices—United
States—Juvenile literature. 5. Lester, Julius—Juvenile literature.
[1. Race awareness. 2. Toleration. 3. Racism. 4. Lester, Julius.]
I. Barbour, Karen, ill. II. Title. E184.A1 L464 2005
305.8'00973—dc21   2002010979
Designed by Stephanie Bart-Horvath ❖ First Edition
22 23 SCP 20

For Malcolm, Hilary, Page and Teddy --J.L.

For Daisy, Jasper, and Nic --K.B.

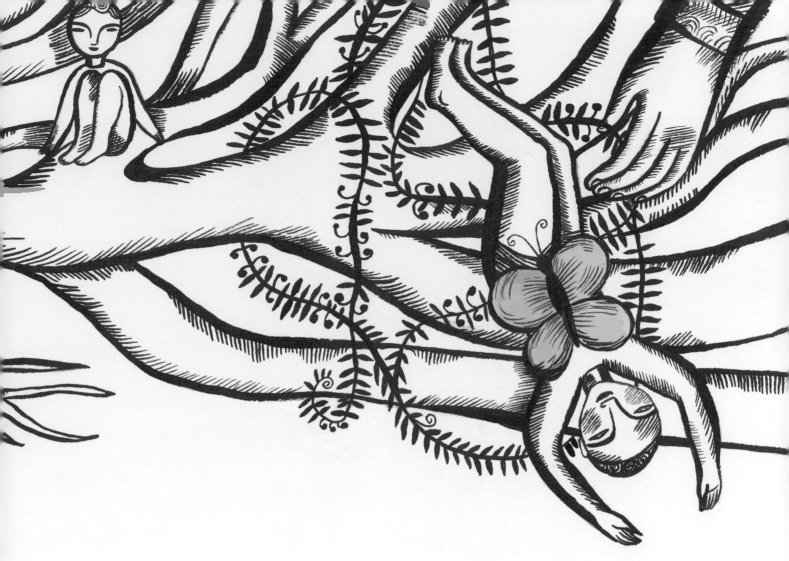

I am a story.
So are you. So is everyone.
My story begins the same way yours does:
"I was born on -------."
Take me, for example.
I was born on January 27, 1939,
in St. Louis, Missouri.
(I'm kind of old, huh?)

HOW DOES YOUR STORY BEGIN?

Many people and many events are part of my story--
and yours, too:
the names of our parents and where they were born,
whether or not we have brothers and/or sisters
(I had a brother who was nine years older than me
but he is dead),
what kind of work our parents do
(or did: my father was a minister;
my mother was a housewife).

My story and yours have many elements, such as

Favorite food: Mine is fish.
Hobbies: I like to do crossword puzzles, take
    photographs and cook.
Favorite color: Red. Or maybe green. But I like
    orange and purple, too. I think my favorite
    color is all of them.
Religion: I'm Jewish.
Nationality: I'm from the United States.
Favorite time of day: Night.

Oh. There's something else

It's part of yours, too.
That's what race we are.

I'm black.

that is part of my story.

What race are you?

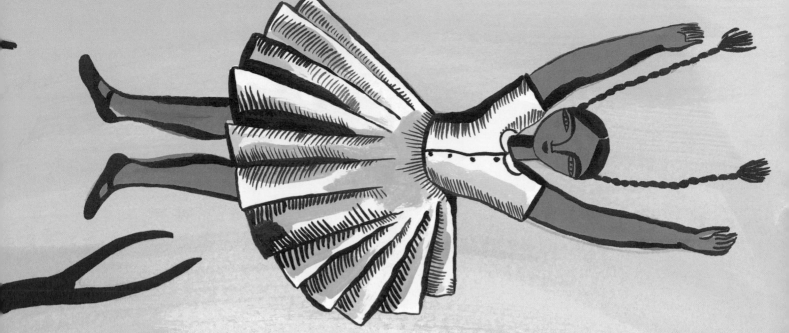

Just as I am a story and you are a story
and countries tell stories
about themselves, race is a story, too.
Whether you're black like me or Asian, Hispanic
or white, each race has a story about itself.
And that story is almost always the same:
"MY RACE IS BETTER THAN YOUR RACE."
Some stories are true. Some are not.
Those who say
"MY RACE IS BETTER THAN YOUR RACE"
are telling a story that is not true.

Why would some people say their race is better than another?

Because
they
feel
bad
about
themselves.
Because
they
are
afraid.

Because.

But there are other ways all of us--even me, even you--think we are better than others.

"I'm better than you because
I live in -------."
"I'm better than you because
I go to ------- School."

"I'm better than you because
I'm a boy."
"I'm better than you because
I'm a girl."
"I'm better than you because
my dad (mom) makes more money
than your dad (mom)."

"I'm better than you
because I'm white."
"I'm better than you
because I'm black."

"I'm better than you
because I'm Hispanic."
"I'm better than you
because I'm Asian."

None of these stories are true.
Are they?

I want to tell a true story. But I need your help.

Here's what I want you to do:

Take your fingers and press them softly against your skin right below your eyes. Be careful and don't poke yourself in the eye.

Okay. Now. Press gently until you feel the hard bone right beneath the surface.

Now, if your mom, dad, brother, sister or a friend is close by, ask them if you can touch them. If they say okay, take your fingers and press softly at the same place beneath their eyes. Press gently until you feel the hard bones right beneath the skin.

Now press someplace else on your body--on your arm, chest, head. Press anywhere until you feel the hard bones beneath your skin.

Beneath everyone's skin are the same hard bones.

If you were to go outside without your skin on and without your hair on your head, turn the page and see what you would look like.

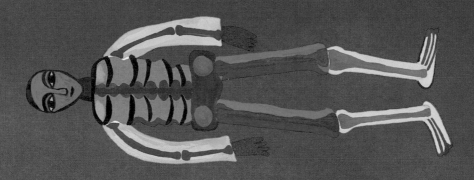

But you want to know something? If I went outside without my skin, my mustache and the hair on my head (what little I have left), I would look just like you. And you would look just like me.

Suppose, just suppose, one day we--I mean everyone in the whole world--decided to take off all our clothes and all our skin and all our hair. Then we would do what we do normally every day--go to school, go to work, play and shop. Everything would be normal except we would look at each other and couldn't tell who was a man, who was a woman, who was white, black, Hispanic or Asian.

Which story shall we believe? The one that says "My race is better than yours"? Or the one we just discovered for ourselves:

Beneath our skin

I look like **you**
and **you** look like
me

and she looks like her
and him
and he looks like him
and her

and we look like them
and they look like us.
When I look at you, which story do I see?

Do I see only:

The **color** of your skin?

The **shape** of your eyes?

The **texture** of your hair?

Do I look at you and think I know your story
when I don't even know your name?
Or, do I look at you and wonder:
What's your name?
When were you born?
Where were you born?
Where do you live?
What do you like?
What don't you like?
Gee, maybe we like and dislike
some of the same things.

Your
race is
not all that
you are. My race
is not all that I am.
Yes, I am black but I am
also a man. I am of medium
height. I have a deep voice and a
loud laugh. (I love to laugh. Do you?)
I live in a big house in the woods in a
small town. I like pancakes and macaroni
and cheese and . . . and . . . and . . .

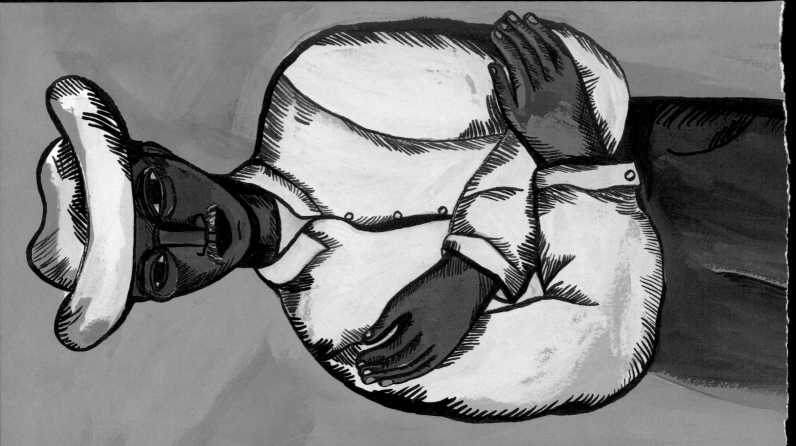

I am so, so, so many things besides my race.
To know my story, you have to put together
everything I am.

(Like I bet you didn't know
I have asthma.)

Beneath the skin we all look alike.

You and Me.

I'll take off my skin.

Will
you
take
off
yours?